Disciplemaking

Living in obedience to the great commission given by Jesus, which entails making more and better followers of Christ

Robert E. Logan

Charles R. Ridley

David J. DeVries

Developed in Partnership

Multiply Vineyard

VINEYARD MISSIONS™

Missional Challenge
Live the Mission!

Published by Missional Challenge

Missional Challenge is committed to advancing disciple making movements globally.

Visit us at **www.missionalchallenge.com**

ISBN: 978-1-939921-34-5

Printed in the United States of America

Acknowledgement

Tara Miller's exceptional writing skills bring our thoughts and ideas to life. Above all others, she makes this book possible. Over many years, her creative collaboration makes it possible to give written resources to the Church so that people can discover and live out their God-given purpose.

CONTENTS

Introduction

God has called—and continues to call—us to a biblical model of discipleship. Discipleship is absolutely foundational to the Vineyard movement. It means following Jesus with all of who we are.

The progression of becoming increasingly more like Jesus—living, loving, serving, helping others become followers of Jesus—is our responsibility as well as our identity as a people.

We live out our discipleship in our words, in our actions, in the presence of community, both those who believe and those who don't.

As disciples on the road to becoming more like Jesus, we yearn for the coming of the Kingdom in all its fullness, the rule and reign of God. We live in the already and the not yet. In community, in scripture, in spiritual formation, in the dynamic work of God among us, we can catch glimpses and tastes of the Kingdom that is yet to come.

As such, we embrace the ongoing process of becoming disciples who make disciples who make disciples. As the yeast mixes through the whole batch of dough, the gospel reproduces itself across the face of the earth. The result is disciples making more disciples making more disciples, then gathering into Kingdom communities called churches.

Discipleship is not something we ever finish in this lifetime. We continue to grow in knowing, being and doing. We progress from an experience of the Holy Spirit, to faith in Jesus, to reconciliation with the Father. We are baptized, we become fishers of men, we obey and teach to obey. We are transformed and transforming. We move toward whole-hearted commitment to God and his Kingdom. The process of discipleship is life-on-life, face-to-face, and hand-in-hand. Together with others, we are invited to join Jesus in the ongoing journey of faith.

Growing in Disciplemaking

Disciplemaking is one of eight discipleship guides for the Vineyard Dimensions of Discipleship series. It doesn't matter which guide you start with—start wherever you'd like and move on to wherever God is leading you next. When we live in the dynamic rhythm and flow of a missional life, we need to take our cues from the Holy Spirit.

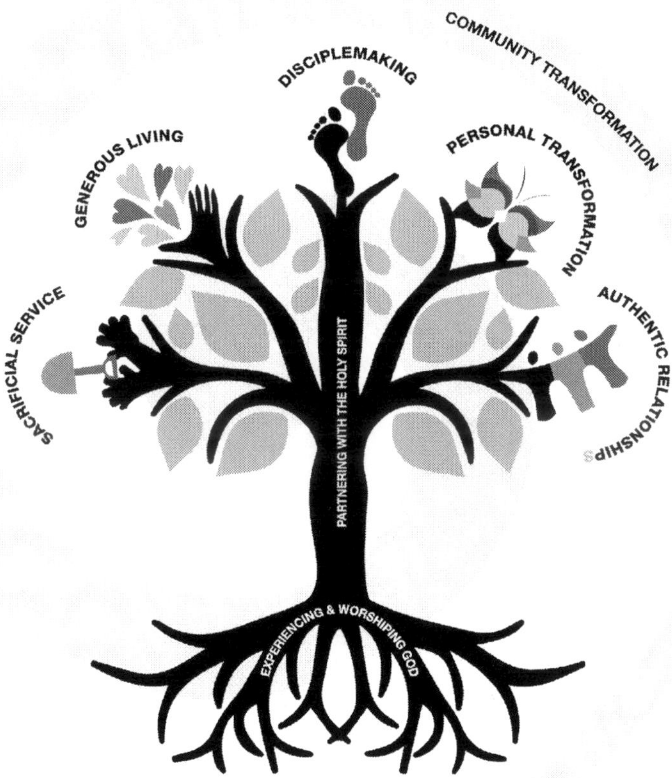

These eight guides are organized according to the tree diagram above; examine it to see how all of the pieces fit together. Disciplemaking is the branch of the tree that holds the means for replicating the entire tree—because we are disciples we in turn make more disciples... who then make more disciples, who go on to make more disciples.

Disciplemaking means living in personal obedience to the great commission given by Jesus, which entails making more and better followers of Christ.

"Therefore, go and make disciples of all the nations, baptizing them in the name of the Father and the Son and the Holy Spirit. Teach these new disciples to obey all the commands I have given you. And be sure of this: I am with you always, even to the end of the age." Matthew 28:19-20

What does it mean to make disciples? Where do we begin? How can we best help others follow Jesus? What pieces need to be in place for the disciplemaking process to replicate itself? The following five-part journey covers these five essential expressions of disciplemaking:

- Deepening concern and compassionate prayer for people without Christ
- Building relationships and trust with people who are not yet followers of Jesus
- Explaining and demonstrating the good news and the way of Jesus
- Connecting people with a Kingdom community of discipleship
- Helping new followers make more followers

> "The greatest act of faith is when a man understands he is not God." —Oliver Wendell Homes, Jr.

Meet together in a group of three or four to talk through each of these expressions. Ask each other these questions. Wait for and listen to responses from the heart. Encourage, challenge, and affirm one another. Go at your own pace: you can do one a week or one a month, whatever pace works best for you. Be sure to allow enough time to live into these behaviors.

Part 1: Deepening concern and compassionate prayer for people without Christ

Key question: *How does concern and compassionate prayer for people without Christ manifest itself in your life?*

If we do not care for people without Christ, we will not make disciples. The rest of the sections of disciplemaking will not make any difference at all if we do not fully engage in this first section: concern, compassion, and prayer.

God the Father modeled that concern by sending his only son to become incarnate and allow us to know him. God the son modeled that by praying for the people and sacrificing himself on the cross that we might come into right relationship with him. The Holy Spirit models that work today by continuing to speak to people in order to draw them near to God. Likewise, we need to model the love of God to others: you can't lead others where you haven't been yourself.

Our role in making disciples is to cooperate with the work that the Holy Spirit is already engaged in. We need to care on a personal level for people who don't know Jesus and we need to pray for them. We need to desire to bring healing to them. Without that foundation, we will not engage in the work of disciplemaking that God has called us to.

This week read and reflect daily on the scripture below. Open a natural flow of conversational prayer with the Holy Spirit as you meditate on the scriptures, inviting him to reveal himself to you. Then gather with those who journey alongside you and interact over the discipleship questions.

Matthew 9:35-38

35 Jesus traveled through all the towns and villages of that area,
teaching in the synagogues and announcing the Good News
about the Kingdom. And he healed every kind of disease and
illness. 36 When he saw the crowds, he had compassion on them
because they were confused and helpless, like sheep without a
shepherd. 37 He said to his disciples, "The harvest is great, but
the workers are few. 38 So pray to the Lord who is in charge of
the harvest; ask him to send more workers into his fields."

Matthew 11:28-30

28 Then Jesus said, "Come to me, all of you who are weary and
carry heavy burdens, and I will give you rest. 29 Take my yoke
upon you. Let me teach you, because I am humble and gentle at
heart, and you will find rest for your souls. 30 For my yoke is
easy to bear, and the burden I give you is light."

Discipleship questions:

- Who that does not know Christ do you feel a deep sense of compassion for?

- How does that compassion manifest itself?

- What blocks you from caring sometimes?

- What connections do you see in Matt 9 (above) between healing, compassion, and discipleship?

- How are you praying for those who don't know Jesus?

"A human being is a part of the whole called by us universe, a part limited in time and space. He experiences himself, his thoughts and feeling as something separated from the rest, a kind of optical delusion of his consciousness. This delusion is a kind of prison for us, restricting us to our personal desires and to affection for a few persons nearest to us. Our task must be to free ourselves from this prison by widening our circle of compassion to embrace all living creatures and the whole of nature in its beauty." —Albert Einstein

Action steps:

- In light of this, what is God asking you to do?

- How will you do this?

- When will you do this?

- Who will help you?

Part 2:
Building relationships and trust with people who are not yet followers of Jesus

Key question: *With whom are you building trusting relationships?*

Too often, Christians build deep, trusting relationships only with one another. Although we may feel safer with people who already agree with us, this is not the model Jesus set forth for us. Our role with those who don't know Jesus is not simply proclaiming the good news, but also engaging with them on an honest relational level.

One of the reasons sharing our faith gets a bad rap is that we are all talk and no listening. No matter what the topic of conversation is, no one enjoys engaging in discipleship with someone who talks the whole time without asking questions of the other person and listening to their answers. It's just basic manners.

Engaging with others through listening and asking questions— and having that same attention returned to us— builds trust and solid relationships. It's also an integral part of people's spiritual journeys. Someone else asking us thought provoking questions and listening to our answers within the context of relationship helps us engage with the ideas in a way we never could by receiving a lecture. This is simply a part of how God has wired us to learn.

As we are sent out into the world to make disciples, we need to engage in numerous conversations along the course of a relationship. It's not one high-stakes meeting where we need to make all the points we want to make. It's a series of conversations where we ask questions and really listen to the answers. And in real conversations, we recognize that not everyone always agrees with us. That's natural. We need to respect the differences and not engage in coercion or cut off the relationship because of disagreements. We can share our perspectives, but we need to recognize that not everyone will agree with us. That's okay—God is still at work in ways we don't understand. Our part is simply to remain faithful in continuing to engage in faith conversations marked by respect.

"Success is the ability to go from one failure to another with no loss of enthusiasm." —Sir Winston Churchill

Questions:

Brainstorm some good, thought-provoking questions that you can ask others when the opportunity arises. Here are a few to get you started:

- What were you taught about God growing up?
- How have you explained death (of, say, a grandparent) to your children?
- What do you find meaningful about your work?

____

____

____

____

This week read and reflect daily on the scripture below. Open a natural flow of conversational prayer with the Holy Spirit as you meditate on the scriptures, inviting him to reveal himself to you. Then gather with those who journey alongside you and interact over the discipleship questions.

John 4:1-26

Jesus knew the Pharisees had heard that he was baptizing and
making more disciples than John 2 (though Jesus himself didn't
baptize them—his disciples did). 3 So he left Judea and
returned to Galilee.

4 He had to go through Samaria on the way. 5 Eventually he
came to the Samaritan village of Sychar, near the field that
Jacob gave to his son Joseph. 6 Jacob's well was there; and Jesus,
tired from the long walk, sat wearily beside the well about
noontime. 7 Soon a Samaritan woman came to draw water, and
Jesus said to her, "Please give me a drink." 8 He was alone at the
time because his disciples had gone into the village to buy
some food.

9 The woman was surprised, for Jews refuse to have anything to do with Samaritans. She said to Jesus, "You are a Jew, and I am a Samaritan woman. Why are you asking me for a drink?"

10 Jesus replied, "If you only knew the gift God has for you and who you are speaking to, you would ask me, and I would give you living water."

11 "But sir, you don't have a rope or a bucket," she said, "and this
well is very deep. Where would you get this living water? 12 And
besides, do you think you're greater than our ancestor Jacob,
who gave us this well? How can you offer better water than he
and his sons and his animals enjoyed?"

13 Jesus replied, "Anyone who drinks this water will soon
become thirsty again. 14 But those who drink the water I give
will never be thirsty again. It becomes a fresh, bubbling spring

within them, giving them eternal life."

15 "Please, sir," the woman said, "give me this water! Then I'll
never be thirsty again, and I won't have to come here to get
water."

16 "Go and get your husband," Jesus told her.

17 "I don't have a husband," the woman replied.

Jesus said, "You're right! You don't have a husband— 18 for you
have had five husbands, and you aren't even married to the
man you're living with now. You certainly spoke the truth!"

19 "Sir," the woman said, "you must be a prophet. 20 So tell me,
why is it that you Jews insist that Jerusalem is the only place of
worship, while we Samaritans claim it is here at Mount
Gerizim, where our ancestors worshiped?"

21 Jesus replied, "Believe me, dear woman, the time is coming
when it will no longer matter whether you worship the Father
on this mountain or in Jerusalem. 22 You Samaritans know very
little about the one you worship, while we Jews know all about
him, for salvation comes through the Jews. 23 But the time is
coming—indeed it's here now—when true worshipers will
worship the Father in spirit and in truth. The Father is looking
for those who will worship him that way. 24 For God is Spirit, so
those who worship him must worship in spirit and in truth."

25 The woman said, "I know the Messiah is coming—the one
who is called Christ. When he comes, he will explain everything
to us."

26 Then Jesus told her, "I Am the Messiah!"

Discipleship questions:

- With whom are you building trusting relationships? How many of those are not yet followers of Jesus?

- How curious are you about the beliefs of others?

- Describe the last time you asked questions about someone's spiritual journey and listened without injecting your own opinion?

- What are the challenges of listening?

- How have people responded when you have listened?

- Where have you sensed the Holy Spirit at work as they've talked?

Action steps:

- In light of this, what is God asking you to do?

- How will you do this?

- When will you do this?

- Who will help you?

Part 3:

Explaining and demonstrating the good news and the way of Jesus

Key question: *How would you explain the good news of Jesus in a few simple sentences? How are you living out that good news?*

> "Make everything as simple as possible, but not simpler."
> —Albert Einstein

Are we to proclaim the gospel with words or with deeds? The answer is simple: both. Jesus did both, and we are to model our actions and our words on his. He showed us how to live and he told us how to live.

A very significant part of what Jesus told us to do was to pass the gospel message on to others. That's disciplemaking at the heart of the great commission. Passing on the gospel to others takes place in two parts: 1) having a clear understanding the basic essentials of what the gospel is, and 2) deciding how best to communicate to others so they too will gain that understanding of the essentials.

The communication was done through both words and deeds. For example, Jesus healed and washed feet, and died on the cross. He also taught and dialogued with people for hours, used many agrarian and fishing examples, as they reflected the culture of the people he was trying to reach.

How might we use modern day examples to explain to others the gospel? How might our modern day lives be an example of the gospel to others?

> "I believe in Christianity as I believe that the sun has risen: not only because I see it, but because by it I see everything else." —C.S. Lewis

This week read and reflect daily on the scripture below. Open a natural flow of conversational prayer with the Holy Spirit as you meditate on the scriptures, inviting him to reveal himself to you. Then gather with those who journey alongside you and interact over the discipleship questions.

Psalm 34:8

8 Taste and see that the Lord is good.
Oh, the joys of those who take refuge in him!

Mark 1:14-15

14 Later on, after John was arrested, Jesus went into Galilee,
where he preached God's Good News. **15** "The time promised by
God has come at last!" he announced. "The Kingdom of God is
near! Repent of your sins and believe the Good News!"

Acts 18:24-28

24 Meanwhile, a Jew named Apollos, an eloquent speaker who
knew the Scriptures well, had arrived in Ephesus from
Alexandria in Egypt. 25 He had been taught the way of the Lord,
and he taught others about Jesus with an enthusiastic spirit
and with accuracy. However, he knew only about John's
baptism. 26 When Priscilla and Aquila heard him preaching
boldly in the synagogue, they took him aside and explained the
way of God even more accurately.

27 Apollos had been thinking about going to Achaia, and the
brothers and sisters in Ephesus encouraged him to go. They
wrote to the believers in Achaia, asking them to welcome him.
When he arrived there, he proved to be of great benefit to those
who, by God's grace, had believed. 28 He refuted the Jews with

powerful arguments in public debate. Using the Scriptures, he explained to them that Jesus was the Messiah.

Colossians 4: 3-4

3 Pray for us, too, that God will give us many opportunities to
speak about his mysterious plan concerning Christ. That is why
I am here in chains. 4 Pray that I will proclaim this message as
clearly as I should.

Discipleship questions:

- What are some essential actions you can take that would demonstrate the gospel to others?

- Describe the gospel in under three minutes as you would to someone who doesn't already understand it.

- What do you understand to be the basic essentials of the gospel?

- Who do you know who needs to consider those essentials?

- How can you best invite that person to do so?

- How can the decision to follow Jesus be made more plain to people?

- Think of someone you are in relationship with. How can you invite them to follow Jesus in a way that will make sense to them?

- How will you balance your intellectual understanding of the essentials with experiential understanding? How will you demonstrate both to people who don't yet know Jesus?

Think of an image

Images—or word pictures—are used throughout scripture. A small seed growing into a large tree. An old wineskin breaking when filled with new wine. A vast field of wheat waiting to be harvested. When you consider the story of the gospel from within your own cultural context, what images come to mind? Choose one and write a paragraph about it.

Action steps:

- In light of this, what is God asking you to do?
- How will you do this?
- When will you do this?
- Who will help you?

Part 4: Connecting people with a Kingdom community of discipleship

Key question: *How can you connect new believers with a Kingdom community that will further their discipleship?*

We need one another. Christianity is not a go-it-alone faith. The way God has set up the church from the beginning is that we are to live out our faith from within a context of community. A new believer must have fellowship of some kind with other believers. That community provides the means of encouragement, challenging, learning, and prayer. Therefore, every time a new believer comes to the faith, they must be connected to the larger body of Christ.

The element of learning from one another is a non-negotiable in discipleship. We cannot learn to become more like Jesus and follow him more faithfully in isolation from others. It's simply not how we were designed as humans, and it certainly is not how Jesus established people in a discipleship process. We are all different parts of the same body and we all bring different gifts to the table. Because of this relational dynamic, no one can disciple another person alone. The full Body of Christ is needed. We can learn things from one another that we cannot learn on our own or from just one other person.

> "Learn from the mistakes of others. You can't live long enough to make them all yourself." —Eleanor Roosevelt

However, there is a dilemma that taking someone out of their natural network of relationships and surrounding them with

Christians can block the continuing path of others coming to faith through that network of relationships. So at the same time that you connect new believers with the body, you also need to ensure that they remain connected to their natural network of friends, family, and co-workers.

> "Every time there is a new convert, you have discovered an elbow, a kneecap, or a nose. The assumption is that the rest of the body must be nearby and a church will emerge through evangelizing the new convert's network of relationships. Through any one person, you can find the seeds of a new church." —Robert E. Logan, *Be Fruitful and Multiply*

This week read and reflect daily on the scripture below. Open a natural flow of conversational prayer with the Holy Spirit as you meditate on the scriptures, inviting him to reveal himself to you. Then gather with those who journey alongside you and interact over the discipleship questions.

Colossians 3:12-17

12 Since God chose you to be the holy people he loves, you must
clothe yourselves with tenderhearted mercy, kindness,
humility, gentleness, and patience. 13 Make allowance for each
other's faults, and forgive anyone who offends you. Remember,
the Lord forgave you, so you must forgive others. 14 Above all,
clothe yourselves with love, which binds us all together in
perfect harmony. 15 And let the peace that comes from Christ
rule in your hearts. For as members of one body you are called
to live in peace. And always be thankful.

16 Let the message about Christ, in all its richness, fill your lives.
Teach and counsel each other with all the wisdom he gives.
Sing psalms and hymns and spiritual songs to God with
thankful hearts. 17 And whatever you do or say, do it as a
representative of the Lord Jesus, giving thanks through him to

God the Father.

Acts 2:42-47

42 All the believers devoted themselves to the apostles'
teaching, and to fellowship, and to sharing in meals (including
the Lord's Supper), and to prayer.

43 A deep sense of awe came over them all, and the apostles
performed many miraculous signs and wonders. 44 And all the
believers met together in one place and shared everything they
had. 45 They sold their property and possessions and shared
the money with those in need. 46 They worshiped together at
the Temple each day, met in homes for the Lord's Supper, and
shared their meals with great joy and generosity— 47 all the
while praising God and enjoying the goodwill of all the people.
And each day the Lord added to their fellowship those who
were being saved.

Acts 16:14-15

14 One of them was Lydia from Thyatira, a merchant of
expensive purple cloth, who worshiped God. As she listened to
us, the Lord opened her heart, and she accepted what Paul was
saying. 15 She was baptized along with other members of her
household, and she asked us to be her guests.

Acts 16:31-34

31 They replied, "Believe in the Lord Jesus and you will be
saved, along with everyone in your household." 32 And they
shared the word of the Lord with him and with all who lived in
his household. 33 Even at that hour of the night, the jailer cared
for them and washed their wounds. Then he and everyone in
his household were immediately baptized. 34 He brought them
into his house and set a meal before them, and he and his
entire household rejoiced because they all believed in God.

Discipleship questions:

- When have you seen a new believer completely submerged into the church? What did that look like? What were the results?

- What are the risks of continuing with their existing network of relationships? What are the possible benefits?

- How can you take a both-and approach?

- What do new believers need from other believers? How can you ensure that is provided?

Action steps:

- In light of this, what is God asking you to do?
- How will you do this?
- When will you do this?
- Who will help you?

Part 5:

Helping new followers make more followers

Key question: *How are you helping new followers of Jesus make more followers of Jesus?*

You could make 100 followers of Jesus, yet if you don't help them go on to make other followers of Jesus, the long-term impact will be small. On the contrary, if you made three followers of Jesus and taught them all to make more followers, and they taught those they discipled to make more disciples, the long-term impact would be significant and far-reaching. Such is the power of multiplication over addition.

Consider the potential of the five step discipleship process. How many followers of Jesus would there be if each current follower engaged a process like this?

- I do - you watch
- I do - you help
- You do - I help
- You do - I watch
- You do - somebody else watches

The personal impact on ourselves is equally significant. God calls us to pour out what he has poured out on us. Because we have been loved, we love. It's contagious. When God is at work in your life, you naturally have something to share with others. In turn, your sharing with others opens you up wider to the work God is doing within you. If we are in relationship with God, we have a story to tell... and that story was meant to be passed on from person to person to person through the generations.

> "But how could you live and have no story to tell?"
> —Fyodor Dostoyevsky, *White Nights*

This week read and reflect daily on the scripture below. Open a natural flow of conversational prayer with the Holy Spirit as you meditate on the scriptures, inviting him to reveal himself to you. Then gather with those who journey alongside you and interact over the discipleship questions.

Acts 16:4-5

4 Then they went from town to town, instructing the believers
to follow the decisions made by the apostles and elders in
Jerusalem. 5 So the churches were strengthened in their faith
and grew larger every day.

Ephesians 4:11-13

11 Now these are the gifts Christ gave to the church: the
apostles, the prophets, the evangelists, and the pastors and
teachers. 12 Their responsibility is to equip God's people to do
his work and build up the church, the body of Christ. 13 This
will continue until we all come to such unity in our faith and
knowledge of God's Son that we will be mature in the Lord,
measuring up to the full and complete standard of Christ.

John 4:39-42

39 Many Samaritans from the village believed in Jesus because
the woman had said, "He told me everything I ever did!"
40 When they came out to see him, they begged him to stay in
their village. So he stayed for two days, 41 long enough for many
more to hear his message and believe. 42 Then they said to the
woman, "Now we believe, not just because of what you told us,
but because we have heard him ourselves. Now we know that

he is indeed the Savior of the world."

Deuteronomy 7:8-9

8 Rather, it was simply that the Lord loves you, and he was
keeping the oath he had sworn to your ancestors. That is why
the Lord rescued you with such a strong hand from your
slavery and from the oppressive hand of Pharaoh, king of
Egypt. 9 Understand, therefore, that the Lord your God is
indeed God. He is the faithful God who keeps his covenant for a
thousand generations and lavishes his unfailing love on those
who love him and obey his commands.

"The greatest single cause of atheism in the world today is Christians: who acknowledge Jesus with their lips, walk out the door, and deny Him by their lifestyle. That is what an unbelieving world simply finds unbelievable."
—Brennan Manning

Discipleship questions:

- What spiritual legacy do you hope to leave?

- How are you challenging those you are discipling to make more disciples?

- How will you ensure that disciplemaking covers multiple generations?

- How are you best equipped to not just make but multiply disciples?

Dollars and cents:

Suppose a father offers his two sons the choice of taking either one dollar a week for 52 weeks or one cent the first week and an amount each week for the next 51 one weeks that is double the previous week's amount. Which one would you choose?

The first choice would just be adding one dollar each week —that's linear growth. At the end of 52 weeks—he'd have $52. The second choice is multiplication—that's exponential growth. If one of the sons chooses this, at the end of the year he will have an unbelievable amount of money. In fact, his allowance in the last week (not the total amount accumulated over 52 weeks) would be $22,517,998,136,852.48. Initially the multiplication is slow, but don't let that deceive you. In the long run, addition never keeps pace with multiplication. Multiplication is explosive.

- What is your vision for future generations of believers?

- What blessings can you pray on the next generation of leaders?

Action steps:

- In light of this, what is God asking you to do?

- How will you do this?

- When will you do this?

- Who will help you?

What's next?

So you've completed this guide. What now? Is there another dimension of discipleship you need to zoom in on? If so, which one?

Because the Vineyard Dimensions of Discipleship guides aren't meant to be used in any particular order, it's up to you to do some listening to the Holy Spirit. Take a look at the big picture and decide where God is leading you next. With a holistic system, it's always a surprise. No matter which guide you choose next, you're engaged in an ongoing action-reflection process as you continue living incarnationally and missionally. All of the Vineyard Dimensions of Discipleship guides are listed below:

- *Experiencing and Worshipping God:* Intentionally and consistently engaging with God in such a way that you open yourself to a deeper relationship with him and his Kingdom
- *Partnering with the Holy Spirit:* Actively listening to the Holy Spirit and taking action according to what you are hearing
- *Sacrificial Service:* Doing good works out of the overflow of God's love and work in our lives
- *Generous Living:* Faithfully stewarding and investing what God has given you so you can contribute toward the advancement of the Kingdom
- *Disciplemaking:* Living in obedience to the great commission given by Jesus, which entails making more and better followers of Christ
- *Personal Transformation:* Experiencing change in your attitudes and behaviors as a result of your relationship with God and others
- *Authentic Relationships:* Engaging with other people in ways that reflect the heart of God toward them
- *Community Transformation:* Personal involvement with others to facilitate positive change where you live and beyond

Maybe what's next isn't another Vineyard Dimensions of Discipleship guide. Here are a few other options:

- If you have a friend or mentor you've been going through these guides with—or if you'd like to begin

- discipling someone, you can greatly increase the fruitfulness of your coaching relationship using www.disciple.mycoachlog.com—a tool to help you stay on track, reflect on what God is doing, and celebrate progress.
- You may be ready to take coaching to the next level by getting a coach, being trained as a coach, or having coach training facilitated for your church. Check out www.missionaltoolkit.com/coaching for more information about these opportunities.
- You can move on to a similar series: The Journey Together Now guides. You can find out more about these downloadable guides at www.journeytogethernow.com.

No matter what's next for you, continue to grow in the ways you follow Jesus into your continuing journey of discipleship.

VINEYARD DISCIPLE ASSESSMENT

Advancing your spiritual development

vineyard.discipleassessment.com

Your church will only grow as well as the disciples that you develop.

Finally - a way to measure progress in discipleship reliably: for individuals, small groups, churches, and missional communities.

The portrait of Jesus in the four gospels serves as our guide. Disciples seek to live and love like Jesus.

The **Vineyard Disciple Assessment** provides a snapshot of where you are in 8 dimensions of following Jesus.

Benefits to your Ministry:

- Every believer discovers growth areas
- Intentional, reproducible discipleship process
- Encourages everyone to live and love like Jesus
- Relational, Spirit-led context for moving forward
- Development of more and better disciples

This **360° assessment** provides feedback that can help you see your own path of discipleship more accurately and more holistically, as well as provide direction for future growth. Your view along with the perspective of friends, family, spiritual leaders, and those you are influencing to follow Jesus will give you **comprehensive feedback on your progress as a disciple.**

Dimensions of Discipleship

After taking the Vineyard Disciple Assessment—discover ways to grow deeper through the Vineyard Dimensions of Discipleship Guides and e-courses.

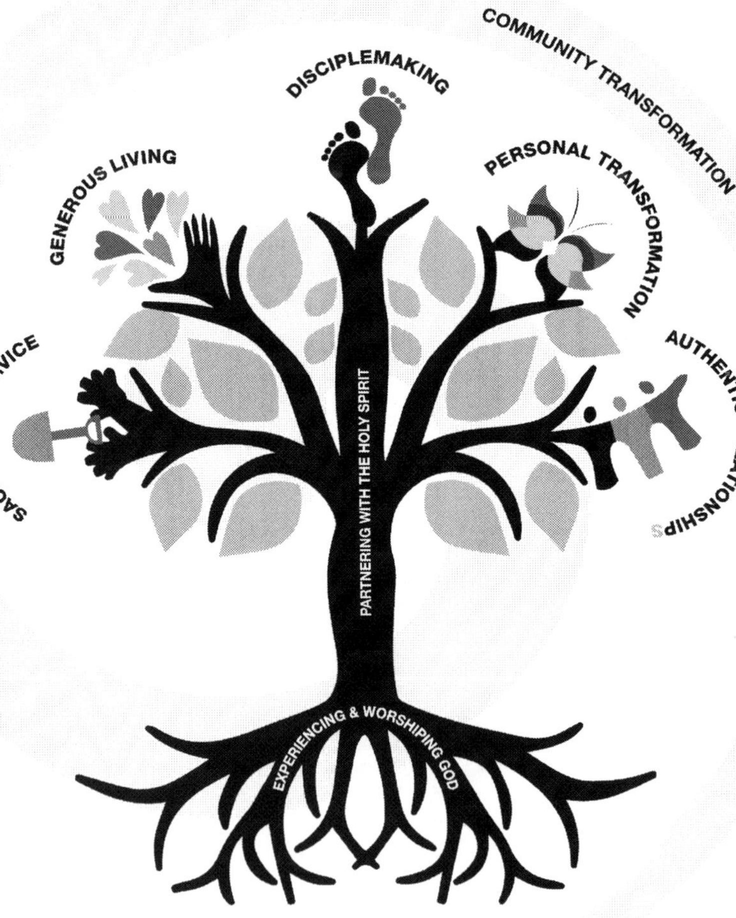

Go to vineyard.discipleassessment.com/resources today.

48955304R00025

Made in the USA
Lexington, KY
19 January 2016